DATE DUE

OEMCO 128-8155

LORDS OF THE SAVANNA

LORDS OF THE SAVANNA

THE BAMBARA, FULANI, IGBO, MOSSI, AND NUPE

PHILIP KOSLOW

CHELSEA HOUSE PUBLISHERS • Philadelphia

Frontispiece: A painted wooden ram mask from the Mossi, Burkina Faso.

On the Cover: An artist's interpretation of a Bambara agrarian mask made of cowrie shells; in the background, the savannas of West Africa.

CHELSEA HOUSE PUBLISHERS
Editorial Director Richard Rennert
Production Manager Pamela Loos
Picture Editor Judy Hasday
Art Director Sara Davis
Senior Production Editor Lisa Chippendale

THE KINGDOMS OF AFRICA
Senior Editor John Ziff

Staff for LORDS OF THE SAVANNA
Project Editor Therese De Angelis
Editorial Assistant Kristine Brennan
Designer Takeshi Takahashi
Picture Researcher Patricia Burns
Cover Illustrator Bradford Brown

First Printing
1 3 5 7 9 8 6 4 2

Library of Congress Cataloging-in-Publication Data

Koslow, Philip.
Lords of the savanna: the Bambara, Fulani, Igbo, Mossi, and Nupe / Philip Koslow.
64 pp.   cm.
Includes bibliographical references and index.
Summary: An historical survey of five peoples of precolonial West Africa, each of which made lasting contributions to art, politics, religion, and other areas.
ISBN 0-7910-3141-1 (hc). — ISBN 0-7910-3142-X (pbk)
1. Ethnology—Africa, West—Juvenile literature. 2. Africa, West—History—Juvenile literature. 3. Africa, West—Social life and customs—Juvenile literature. [1. Ethnology—Africa, West. 2. Africa, West—History. 3. Africa, West—Social life and customs.] I. Title.
GN652.5.K67 1997
305.8'00966—dc21   97-7295

CONTENTS

The Cradle of Humanity   7

1 "Civilization and Magnificence"   11

2 Fighters for the Faith   19

Masks and Ceremony - *Picture Essay*   25

3 Pioneers of Democracy   31

The Art of the Savanna - *Picture Essay*   37

4 Kingdom of the Sun   43

5 The Chain of Tsoede   51

Chronology   56

Further Reading   58

Glossary   60

Index   62

Titles in
THE KINGDOMS OF AFRICA

ANCIENT GHANA
  The Land of Gold

MALI
  Crossroads of Africa

SONGHAY
  The Empire Builders

KANEM-BORNO
  1,000 Years of Splendor

YORUBALAND
  The Flowering of Genius

HAUSALAND
  The Fortress Kingdoms

BENIN
  Lords of the River

SENEGAMBIA
  Land of Lion

DAHOMEY
  The Warrior Kings

ASANTE
  The Gold Coast

LORDS OF THE SAVANNA
  The Bambara, Fulani,
  Igbo, Mossi and Nupe

BUILDING A NEW WORLD
  Africans in America,
  1500–1900

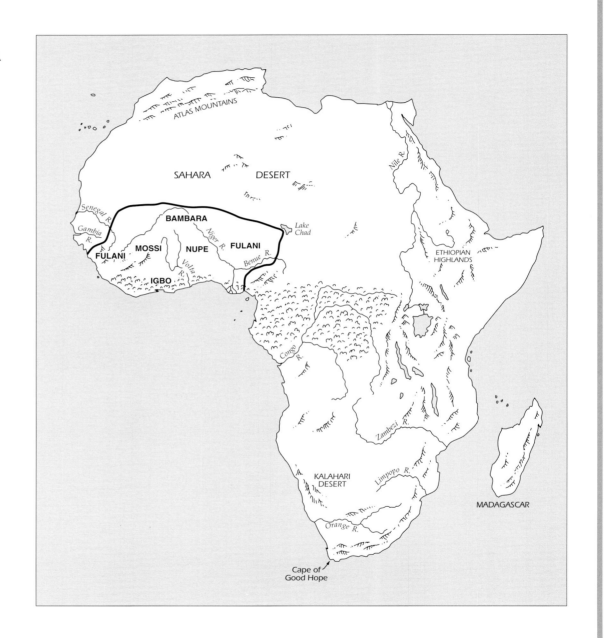

THE CRADLE OF HUMANITY

At the end of the 19th century, when the European powers were ruthlessly carving Africa into colonies, Professor H. E. Egerton of England's Oxford University declared that African history before the arrival of Europeans had been nothing more than "blank, uninteresting, brutal barbarism." This view, common in Europe, rationalized the Europeans' increasing exploitation of the African continent. If, as the professor claimed, Africans had lived in chaos throughout their history, Europeans could believe they were doing a noble deed by imposing their will and their way of life upon Africa.

7

Today Egerton's views are useful only to illustrate the monumental arrogance and ignorance of 19th-century colonialists. Since the end of World War II in 1945, when independence movements arose throughout Africa, unbiased scholars from many nations have pursued intensive studies of African history and African culture. These efforts took on added significance when most Africans won their freedom from colonial rule around 1960 and endeavored to build new political systems upon ancient foundations. Though the field of African studies is still in its infancy, it has already uncovered the richness of Africa's past and its crucial role in world history.

The story of humanity begins in Africa: about 7.5 million years ago, the first humanlike creatures, known as hominids, appeared on the African continent and gradually evolved into *Homo sapiens*, the species to which all human beings belong. About 150,000 years ago, *Homo sapiens* began spreading through the rest of the

A relief map of Africa indicating the territories of the Bambara, Fulani, Igbo, Mossi, and Nupe peoples.

This terra-cotta head is one of the many treasures of the Nok culture, a highly sophisticated West African people who flourished during the 5th century B.C.

world from Africa. Thus, in a very real sense, present-day peoples of all races and nationalities share a common heritage—and that heritage is decidedly African.

As early as the 5th century B.C., dark-skinned peoples living in West Africa had developed highly sophisticated ways of life. At this time, the Nok culture arose in the central portion of present-day Nigeria. The artists of Nok produced numerous sculptures that were lost for many centuries then rediscovered during the 1930s. These striking figures, most of which represent human heads, have a stylistic beauty and emotional power that place them among the world's greatest works of art.

By A.D. 750, West Africa's first great kingdom, ancient Ghana, had achieved vast wealth by controlling the gold trade between North Africa and the Sudan. (The regions south of the Sahara Desert were known to North African traders as Bilad al-Sudan, "the land of the black peoples.") When ancient Ghana began to decline during the 12th century, its role as a regional power passed to the great empires of Mali and Songhay, whose domains extended along the mighty Niger

River and across the rolling plains of the West African savanna. Ironically, the enormous gold supplies of Mali and Songhay enabled the nations of Europe to emerge from a long period of decline and to embark on an age of expansion, ultimately at the expense of Africa's sovereignty.

Although Mali and Songhay were the largest kingdoms of precolonial Africa, a host of other states rivaled them in military power, political sophistication, and cultural achievement. Among these were Kanem-Borno, whose royal dynasty reigned for 1,000 years on the shores of Lake Chad; the fortress kingdoms of Hausaland, whose armored horsemen vied for supremacy on the sun-baked plains of Nigeria; the forestland states of Yorubaland and Benin, where artistic skill and religious devotion combined to produce countless masterpieces; and Asante, whose gold-rich civilization was unsurpassed in the arts of commerce, diplomacy, and war.

Together, the chronicles of these great kingdoms still make up only a fraction of Africa's historical wonders. More than 800 ethnic groups flourish on the African continent, each possessing its own record of achievement. Among this vast constellation are five West African peoples who exemplify the wide range of African culture and history: the Bambara of Mali; the Igbo of southeastern Nigeria; the Mossi of Burkina Faso; the Nupe of northern Nigeria; and the nomadic Fulani, whose migrations have often changed the face of Africa.

Chapter 1 | "CIVILIZATION AND MAGNIFICENCE"

Mali workers cultivate the land. The Bambara ceremony of the chi wara *encouraged every farmer to strive for strength and endurance in the challenging environment of the West African savanna.*

In years past, when the summer rains began to fall on the parched West African savanna and farmers began the all-important task of planting their crops, many Bambara villages were invaded by a bizarre pair of creatures. Emerging suddenly from the bush, the strange beasts sported antelope horns but walked on two legs rather than four. Masses of long black fibers, reaching down to the ground, covered their heads and bodies. They moved quickly about the village square, furrowing the ground with short sticks. As the excited villagers sang and clapped, the two-legged antelopes worked for hours, sometimes performing acrobatic leaps or emitting high-pitched yelps. Finally, at the end of the afternoon, the creatures paused, removed their headgear, and revealed themselves as members of the community.

The Bambara (also known as the Bamana) created this powerful ceremony to evoke the spirit of the *chi wara*, a being that was half human and half antelope. According to traditional beliefs, the chi wara appeared among the Bambara at the beginning of their history and taught them how to plant crops. Thus, the ideal of every Bambara farmer was to emulate the power and endurance of the chi wara by laboring for as long as necessary without complaint or fatigue.

Farming has always been essential to the Bambara's survival in a challenging environment where withering heat can alternate with torrential rain. The Bambara have been established in the vicinity of the middle Niger since ancient times. For centuries, they lived in scattered communities with no central authority. But their social structure began to change during the 12th century, when they were joined by groups of Soninke. The Soninke had founded ancient Ghana during the 8th century, and when their kingdom began to dissolve, many of them migrated to Bamana country.

The languages of the two peoples were similar: both Soninke and Bamanakan belong to the Mande language family, the dominant linguistic group of West Africa, so it was fairly simple for the Soninke to learn Bamanakan and merge with their hosts. Soninke culture also had a profound effect upon the Bambara.

Before the Soninke arrived, Bambara communities were organized around clans, groups of individuals who traced their descent to a common ancestor. The Soninke, on the other hand, were accustomed to living under chiefs and kings who held sway over large territories, commanding allegiance from numerous villages and clan leaders. Clearly, the Bambara were convinced that the political systems of the Soninke could be beneficial, because chiefdoms began to

arise in a number of Bambara territories after the Soninke merged with them.

During the 13th century, the entire Niger region came under the control of the kings of Mali and Songhay. Following the decline of Mali, the even greater empire of Songhay held sway over the lands of the Bambara. In order avoid conquest, the Bambara had to pay an annual tribute, in the form of crops or slaves, to the emperors of the more powerful states. By the 16th century, however, as Songhay was crumbling under the onslaught of North Africans from Morocco, the Bambara began to throw off the empire's yoke and expand their own sphere of influence. Tayiru Banbera, a 20th-century Bambara chronicler, describes these early years as a heroic age:

> In those days the world was not like
>   it is now.
> They bent the world like a scythe,
> And unrolled it like a road.
> They walked the four directions of
>   the world,
> And settled at its center.
> In those days the word of a human
>   being could be trusted.
> There was nobility then.
> If nobles swore an oath, they would
>   say "I am serious,
> It is the word of a noble."

An ancient shrine in the town of Ka-ba, Mali, where the victorious 13th-century king of Mali, Sundiata, met with his commanders and organized the government of his kingdom. During this period, the Bambara gradually abandoned their own social structures and adopted the chiefdom system of the Soninke, with whom they had merged.

13

They pledged their honor.
If a noble swore such an oath, that
  was all.
He would be sure to make it good.

The Bambara finally emerged as a powerful force under the leadership of Biton Kulibali, who in 1712 succeeded to the kingship of Segu, a major city on the Niger. A fearsome warrior known as the "man-killing hunter," Biton Kulibali led his troops in a series of successful campaigns against neighboring towns and villages. In these battles, the Bambara employed maneuvers they had

14

The great mosque of Jenne, built in the 14th century on an island in the Bani River, a tributary of the Niger, is still in use today. Mali rulers adopted Islam during the 13th century and required tribute in the form of crops or slaves from the Bambara. Though the Bambara eventually gained independence, they battled for centuries against Fulani Muslims determined to spread Islam throughout West Africa.

developed in one of their favorite pastimes, the game of *nperi*. Though similar to checkers, nperi was originally played not on a board but within a square drawn on the ground. While moving their pieces, the Bambara devised strategies for defeating their enemies. As Tayiru Banbera explains:

> You must know how to approach the
>   enemy town,
> You must know how to get away
>   from it.
> Oh, the way the opposing forces
>   would confront each other,
> That was planned according to
>   moves in the house of *nperi*.

After the death of Biton Kulibali, Bambara warriors continued their onslaught under the banner of Ngolo Jara (1766-87), who conquered the great trading centers of Jenne and Timbuktu and became the undisputed master of the middle Niger. Ngolo Jara left his son Monzon an empire that filled the void left by Mali and Songhay. When the Scottish explorer, Mungo Park, reached Segu in July 1796, he was astonished by what he saw:

> Sego, the capital of Bambarra . . .
> consists, properly speaking, of four
> distinct towns. . . . They are all sur-

rounded with high mud-walls; the houses are built of clay, of a square form, with flat roofs; some of them have two stories, and many of them are whitewashed. Besides these buildings, Moorish mosques are seen in every quarter; and the streets, though narrow, are broad enough for every useful purpose, in a country where wheel carriages are entirely unknown. From the best inquiries I could make, I have reason to believe that Sego contains altogether about thirty thousand inhabitants. . . . The view of this extensive city, the numerous canoes upon the river; the crowded population; and the cultivated state of the surrounding country, formed altogether a prospect of civilization and magnificence, which I little expected to find in the bosom of Africa.

Park could explore no further, because Monzon refused to allow him into the city. Segu was home to many Muslims, followers of the religion of Islam; Muslims and Christians had been at odds for centuries, and Monzon apparently feared that Park would be attacked. (Indeed, Park had been captured by a group of Muslims earlier in his travels and had barely escaped with his life.) When he learned that Park was out of money, Monzon sent him a large sum to buy provisions for the rest of his journey. Though disappointed that he could not meet Monzon, Park believed that the king's actions were "prudent and liberal." He would undoubtedly have understood the lamentation of Segu's bards upon Monzon's death in 1808:

> The day is ending,
> The ground is hot.
> We have no basket to sit on in the sky
> While we tell our troubles to the
>   angels of God.

Though Segu never again had a ruler as able as Monzon, the kingdom remained strong and prosperous under his heirs.

By the middle of the 19th century, however, the Bambara domains were in grave danger from the advance of Fulani Muslim troops who were determined to spread Islam throughout West Africa. The great Muslim commander Umar Tal launched a triumphant jihad (holy war) against the Bambara state of Kaarta in 1855 and attacked Segu four years later. Though superior in numbers, Segu's forces could not match the impassioned fury of the Muslim troops, who reviled their enemies as "the asses of filth" and "the armies of Satan" and rode into battle shouting, "God is helping us, let the

16

pagans be destroyed." Within two years, Segu was in Muslim hands.

Refusing to accept Muslim rule, the Bambara mounted a series of revolts that succeeded only in disrupting trade and farming along the middle Niger, leaving the region vulnerable to Europeans, who were now competing for colonies in Africa. For nearly 20 years, the Bambara and Fulani alike used both arms and diplomacy to thwart the ambitions of the French government, but by 1890 France occupied Segu. Shortly thereafter, the Bambara domains became part of the colony known as French West Africa.

Ultimately, the Bambara survived both conquest and colonialism. Today they number 1.5 million and continue to live along the middle Niger, in the west-central portion of the Republic of Mali. In recent times, as more and more Bambara have converted to Islam, ancient religious ceremonies such as the dance of the chi wara have been abandoned. But as the Bambara and other Malians continue to wrest a living from land that is often ravaged by droughts, the legacy of the chi wara is more important than ever. In modern Mali, the title of chi wara is bestowed upon farmers who work their fields each day without fatigue or complaint, providing an example for the rest of the community. In this way the Bambara have adapted their glorious past to a challenging present.

Chapter 2 | FIGHTERS FOR THE FAITH

A Fulani woman in Mali, 1962. Because the Fulani often differ in appearance from other West African peoples, it is believed that some of their ancestors were Berbers or Arabs.

In the numerous West African countries in which they have settled, the Fulani stand out dramatically. They are generally taller and more slender than other West Africans. Their skin is usually lighter and they have longer, narrower noses. Because of these physical differences, many non-African historians during the past two centuries have theorized that the Fulani have a different origin than their fellow West Africans. At various times, historians have speculated that the Fulani descended from North African Berbers, Middle Eastern Syrians and Jews, East Asian Hindus, and even Polynesians from the Pacific Islands. During the colonial era, many Europeans asserted that the Fulani were descended from a vanished group of people known as Hamites, who had

established all of Africa's historical kingdoms before intermingling with their subjects.

Modern scholars reject the Hamitic theory and other far-fetched hypotheses about Fulani origins. Studies of African language structures show that the Fulani tongue, known as Fulfulde, is similar to languages spoken on Africa's West Atlantic coast. This indicates a decided kinship between the Fulani and other black African peoples such as the Wolof and Serer. Most likely, the Fulani (also known as Fula, Felata, Fulbe, and Peul) descended from groups who raised cattle at the southern edge of the Sahara Desert as early as 5,000 years ago. These peoples may have included individuals of Berber or Arab stock, which would explain the relatively light

A West African herdsman crosses the savanna. As early as 5,000 years ago, the Fulani raised cattle at the edge of the Sahara desert. By the 9th century, the Fulani had moved into the grasslands of West Africa, where they eventually settled as farmers.

20

skin tone of many Fulani. The Fulanis' slenderness and thin facial features may simply be adaptations to the hot, dry environment of their original home.

It is not known exactly when the Fulani began moving south from the edge of the desert into the grasslands of the West African savanna. The first historical record of their presence in the area comes from a 9th-century Arab chronicle. At this time, the Fulani were established in the kingdom of Takrur, just south of the Sahara. Takrur was the first West African state visited by Muslim traders from West Africa, and many of the Fulani who settled as farmers in Takrur adopted the religion of Islam. On the other hand, the cattle-breeding Fulani who began to spread from Takrur to other regions of West Africa tended to observe traditional religions, worshiping their ancestors and the spirits of nature rather than Allah, the supreme being of Islam.

In addition to facing the difficulties of breeding, raising, and feeding their cattle, the wandering Fulani herders sometimes aroused the enmity of those whose territories they crossed. The herders' need for large tracts of grazing land often angered local farmers who wanted the land for planting crops. As a result, many West African rulers strictly limited the Fulanis' grazing privileges or forced them to pay heavy taxes for the right to pasture their herds. Some rulers, such as Sunni Ali, who led the mighty Songhay empire during the late 15th century, went even further. According to a Songhay chronicle, "There was no enemy [Sunni Ali] hated more than the Fulani, and he could not set eyes on a Fulani without killing that person, whether learned or ignorant, man or woman. . . . He decimated the tribe of the Sangare [a Fulani clan] until nothing remained of them but a tiny fraction, which could be gathered in the shade of a single tree."

Fleeing Sunni Ali's wrath, some Fulani migrated westward toward Senegambia on the Atlantic coast. There they joined other groups of Fulani who had been living in the area since the 10th century, in Fouta Djallon, Massina, and Fouta Toro. With this influx of new members, the Fulani communities steadily grew more powerful. By the late 15th century, they were ready to assert themselves as conquerors.

Under the leadership of Tengella and his son Koly, Fulani armies campaigned throughout Senegambia between 1481 and 1514. Their chief opponents were the Mandingo, the powerful horse warriors who formed the backbone of the Mali empire. Despite their military prowess, the Mandingo were no match for the Fulani armies, who presented an awe-inspiring spectacle with their numerous horses and camels and the huge herds of cattle they drove before them. They swept through the savanna like a force of nature, undeterred by political or geographical boundaries. In one campaign, when the Fulani advance was checked by the two-mile-wide Gambia River, the commanders ordered each soldier to find a stone and place it in the water. According to tradition, the Fulani host was so immense that the stones quickly filled the riverbed, allowing the Fulani to thunder across and rout their foes. The place of their crossing has been known ever since that feat as the Fulani Ford.

21

Although the Fulani were later known as staunch Muslims, all the states they established during their first great expansion were founded on traditional tribal religions. Indeed, many Fulani rulers were known to persecute fellow Fulani who had converted to Islam. This situation persisted until the 17th century, when large groups of Muslim Fulani migrated to Fouta Djallon and convinced their brethren that Islam was superior to ancestral beliefs. During the following century, the Fulani Muslims launched the first of the great jihads that would transform the face of West Africa.

The 18th-century jihads erupted first in Fouta Djallon (1725) and then in Fouta Toro (1776); in both cases, Fulani Muslims overthrew the non-Muslim Fulani kings who had once oppressed them. Following these conquests, Fulani Muslims living in Massina rose up against the kingdom's Bambara ruler and established an Islamic state. The new ruler of Massina, Amadu Sisi, was so fierce in his faith that he even destroyed Muslim houses of worship whose services did not meet his standard of purity.

The greatest of all the Fulani jihads occurred in the central Sudan during the early 19th century, under the leadership of Usuman dan Fodio, known to his followers simply as the Shehu, or Teacher. The Shehu was a native of Gobir, one of the leading Hausa states, and belonged to the Torodbe clan, who were known for their strict adherence to Islam. Though the rulers of Gobir and the other Hausa states called themselves Muslims, the Torodbe looked upon them with scorn. In the eyes of the Torodbe, the Hausa rulers practiced a corrupt form of Islam and lived in excessive luxury at the expense of their subjects. The Shehu, in contrast, lived a life of stark simplicity, supporting himself as a rope maker while he taught and preached; it was said that he owned nothing but a pair of trousers, a turban, and a robe.

By 1804, tensions between the Shehu's followers and the ruler of Gobir erupted into an all-out war. The bitterly contested struggle spread throughout Hausaland and raged until 1812, when the Torodbe-led *mudjahidun* (fighters for the faith)— who had among them many Hausa, Wolof, Mandingo, and North African Tuaregs as well as Fulani— emerged victorious.

The Shehu then organized an Islamic empire with two provinces: the Sokoto

22

Caliphate in the north and the Emirate of Gwandu in the south. After the Shehu's death in 1817, Sokoto (the dominant province) was ruled by his son Muhammad Bello. Following their triumphant jihad, the Fulani had vowed to create an ideal Islamic government that would provide justice for all citizens. Although they fell short of that ambitious goal, they did achieve genuine reforms in Sokoto and Gwandu. For instance, the Fulani freed many slaves as a reward for their support, and a number of these individuals came to occupy important posts in government. In general, the strong regime stabilized the region and stimulated trade and commerce in the central Sudan. The benefits of this boom extended to Fulani and non-Fulani peoples alike.

Not surprisingly, the stunning success of the Shehu's jihad further galvanized Fulani Muslims throughout West Africa. In the western Sudan, the banner of the faith was taken up by Umar Tal, who incorporated the entire middle Niger into a vast Islamic realm known as the Torodbe (or Tukulor) Empire. Thus, the two greatest West African realms of the 19th century were created and governed by Fulani.

The Torodbe Empire was even more

By the 19th century, European powers—Britain and France in particular—were competing for influence in Africa by seizing the territories of African empires. This illustration depicts the gun-train of a British invading force in 1868.

diverse than Sokoto and Gwandu. It consisted of numerous provinces, each one anchored by a heavily fortified city. Though the provinces were highly independent, they were invariably governed by Muslim law. Judges known as *qadis* were known to be severe and unbending; even high officials were flogged if they broke the commandments of the Koran, Islam's holy book.

In his imperial capital at Segu, Umar Tal ruled with the aid of a council of *talibs*, advanced students of Islam. The talibs were drawn from a wide range of ethnic groups and social classes, and their ranks included both princes and slaves. By providing a major political role for learned individuals, the Fulani empires differed markedly from more traditional regimes, in which a council of high-born nobles formed the core of the government. Under Umar, birth status mattered little; the primary requirements for power were intellectual ability and a strict observance of Islam.

Umar bequeathed a flourishing empire to his son Ahmadu, who ruled effectively until the 1870s. By that

A Fulani woman, wearing traditional brilliantly colored robes and large gold earrings, weaves straw into mats to be sold at market.

(Continued on page 29)

24

MASKS AND CEREMONY

In his book *The Arts of Black Africa*, art historian Jean Laude explains the importance of masks in various African ceremonies: "A mask is a being that protects the wearer. It is designed to absorb the life-force that escapes from a human being or from an animal at the moment of death."

A Mali mask worn during agrarian dances, made of cowrie shells, beads, and hair. This type of shell was the primary form of currency for residents of the Songhay during the 16th century.

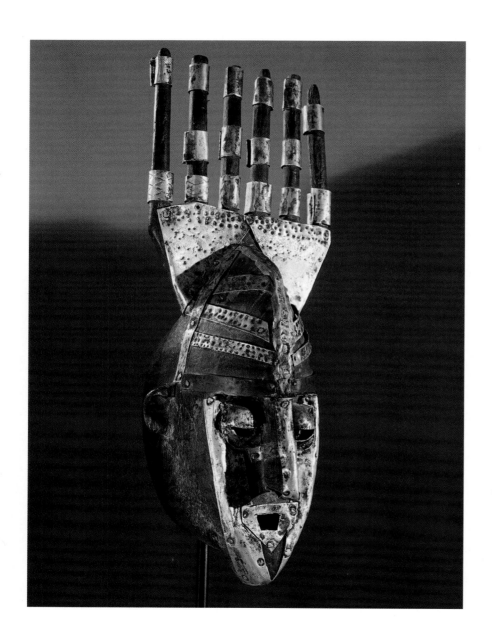

A Ndomo mask of wood and metal, used in dances of the lower grades of male societies among the northern Bambara and the neighboring Marka.

Carved wooden headgear incorporating the antelope figure of the chi wara, *worn by a member of the Tyi-wara society of Mali during agrarian dances.*

A wooden chi wara *sculpture of the Bambara period.*

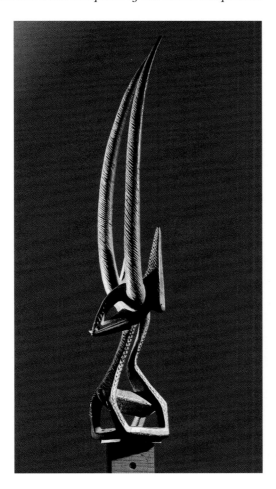

A Mali dancing helmet.

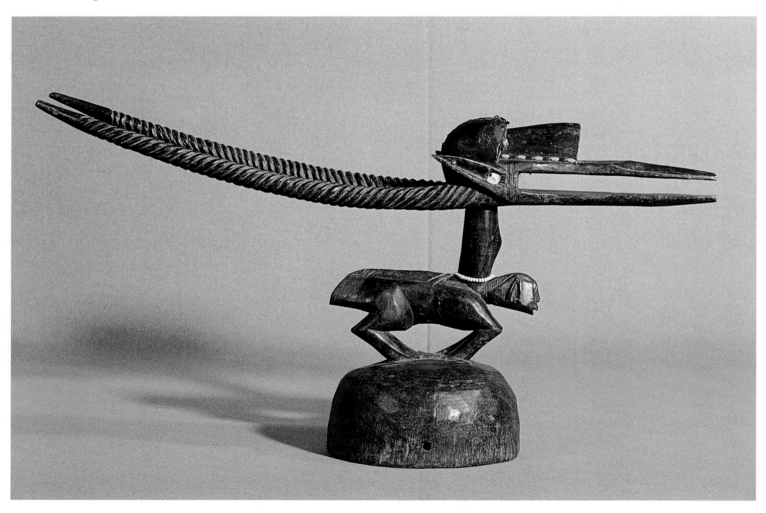

(Continued from page 24)

time, the European powers were competing for influence in Africa, with the French being especially active along the Niger. At first, Ahmadu attempted to accommodate the intruders by granting them certain privileges in exchange for military equipment. When it became clear, however, that France was bent on seizing territory in Africa, Ahmadu fought it with all the resources at his command.

The superior weaponry of the French ultimately overcame Torodbe resistance. Ahmadu went into exile in 1891, and the Torodbe domains were later absorbed into French West Africa. Meanwhile, in the east, Sokoto and Gwandu broke up under British pressure, and its provinces became part of the British colony of Nigeria. But the British did retain the Muslim governors of the former Hausa states, and their authority continued through British rule into the independence that eventually followed.

After the nations of West Africa won their independence, the Fulani remained widespread and influential. Today there are important Fulani communities in the nations of Burkina Faso, Ghana, Gambia, Mauritania, Niger, Nigeria, and Senegal. The total Fulani population in the Sudan exceeds five million. Cattle raising continues to be the main livelihood of the Fulani; though some also farm, most continue to lead nomadic lives. Traveling throughout the savanna with their great herds, they trade hides, milk, and cheese for cereals and fish. In market towns they visit with their wares, Fulani women are often easily recognized by their brilliantly colored robes and massive gold earrings, which dramatically illustrate the style and prosperity of this indomitable people.

29

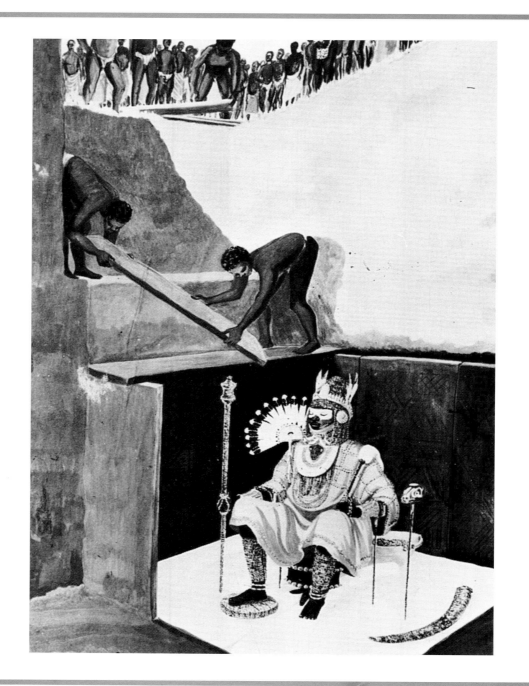

Chapter 3 | PIONEERS OF DEMOCRACY

An archaeologist's reconstruction of the burial chamber of an Igbo ese nri, or religious figure, from the 9th century. The site is in Igbo-Ukwu in present-day southeastern Nigeria.

In 1960, a team of archaeologists led by Thurstan Shaw began to dig in the family compound of Richard Anozie, a farmer in Igbo-Ukwu, in southeastern Nigeria. About 12 feet beneath the surface, they uncovered a large chamber containing various finely crafted objects, including a copper crown, a bronze leopard's head, and armlets made of blue glass beads. After studying the site, Shaw and his colleagues concluded that the chamber had once contained the remains of an important dignitary. The deceased had been placed in a sitting position on a ceremonial stool, dressed in handsome robes, and arrayed in the regalia of his office. The top of the tomb had been secured with timbers and then covered with earth.

In the case of almost any other West African people, it would have been clear that the chamber had been constructed to house the remains of a powerful king. But Shaw and his colleagues knew that the Igbo people (also known as Ibo) had never lived under kings or chiefs. Instead, they had governed themselves with a village-based decision-making process similar to the New England town meetings of colonial America. To unlock the secret of the Igbo-Ukwu tomb, the archaeologists analyzed the unique history of the people who had built it.

The scholars knew that black Africans had occupied the territory of present-day Nigeria for tens of thousands of years and that people identified (largely through language) as Igbo had lived in southeastern Nigeria for at least

The Igbo were exceptionally skilled in design and metalworking techniques. This ceremonial bronze wine bowl from the 9th century is an example of the magnificent treasures unearthed at the Igbo-Ukwu site.

5,000 years. Like a number of neighboring peoples, such as the Edo and the Yoruba, the Igbo have historically depended on farming for their existence, with their staple crop being yams. The similarities end there, however.

Early in their history, the Edo and Yoruba, who lived west of the Niger, began to live in fortified communities separate from their farms, following chiefs and other powerful figures who could organize and lead military forces. In time, the chiefdoms developed into full-scale kingdoms, such as Ife, Oyo, and Ilorin in Yorubaland and Benin in Edo country.

Since the territory east of the Niger was fairly peaceful, Igbo farmers felt no need to organize for self-defense. Instead, each village included a group of men who were skilled at warfare; during the dry season, after the yams had been harvested and stored in barns, these warriors fought for glory and honor rather than conquest. Thus, Igboland enjoyed comparative stability under a very simple form of government. Only in the far west, where peoples from Benin migrated into Igboland, did Igbo communities—notably Aboh, Onitsha, and Aguta—establish traditional kingdoms.

Throughout Igboland, villages were

organized around clans, each one composed of families living in adjoining compounds. Normally the eldest member of the clan acted as the leader, enforcing religious observances and settling disputes between individuals and families. Issues affecting the entire village would be discussed by a council of clan leaders. When a group of villages had a common problem, each one was usually represented by the leader of its largest clan, though any agreement he made had to be acceptable to all of the villagers. In 1973, Noo Odala, a 102-year-old Igbo residing in the village of Umuaga, described a typical village meeting to an interviewer:

> Each person was free to talk during the deliberations, but bad contributions were jeered at with occasional embarrassing shouts of *Di anyi, tukwunyo* (our colleague, sit down). Good contributions were widely acclaimed with occasional clappings and shouts of *Okwu ghi di mma* (your speech is good). In most cases, the reaction of those present helped us to know the acceptable line of action. But it was still necessary that the *onye ishi ani* [village elder] should give the verdict, but within what the people in general had agreed.

In order for this democratic system to work as well as it did, all the Igbo had to agree on a set of guiding principles, and the consequences of breaking the rules had to be enforced. In traditional kingships, the ruler's military might often represented the final authority; among the Igbo, religion took the place of royal decree.

Spiritual authority in Igboland emanated from Nri, known as the Holy City. At Nri, the Igbo had first begun to worship Chukwu, the creative force of the world that is present in every aspect of life. At some point in the past, a citizen of Nri was given the honorary title of *eze;* he was considered the human representative of Chukwu and recognized as the spiritual head of the Igbo. In 1967, Nwaokoye Odenigbo, a leading citizen of Nri, explained to an interviewer how the eze nri used his power:

> Nri got yam, cocoyam, vegetables and palm trees from *Chukwu* and gave them to the Igbo people. *Chukwu* revealed the secret of the year to Nri and showed the four market days to the *Eze Nri* who brought them to the Igbo people. The *Eze Nri* allocated to each Igbo village around, specific functions and jobs. Nri people became priests and administrators,

33

34

Awka became the blacksmiths, Umudioka became the carvers of ritual objects and things.

Using this knowledge, archaeologists solved the mystery of the Igbo-Ukwu tomb. The man buried beneath Richard Anozie's compound had been an eze nri or similar religious figure, revered solely for his command of the spiritual power that bound all Igbo communities. This power inspired remarkable achievements over the centuries. At Igbo-Ukwu, for example, Shaw and his colleagues not only discovered the burial chamber but also unearthed hundreds of magnificent bronze castings. The sculpted heads, jewelry, urns, and *calabashes* (shallow vessels used to hold food and water) have been dated to the 9th century A.D., making them considerably older than comparable (and better-known) works from Benin and Yoruba-land. They also show an exceptional level of skill, both in design and in metalworking technique.

The artistic output of the Igbo communities depended on their ability to grow plentiful crops and to exchange goods with their northern neighbors, such as the Hausa states and Kanem-Borno, who in turn traded with the Muslims of North Africa. From the north, the Igbo obtained salt, glass beads, and textiles as well as copper and other metals for use in their crafts. In exchange, the Igbo exported ivory, kola nuts, and slaves.

The Igbo obtained slaves from a number of sources: prisoners of war, condemned criminals, individuals suspected of practicing witchcraft, or poor families who might be forced to sell one or more children into servitude in order to survive. Traditionally, the slave trade was practiced on a fairly modest scale.

After 1650, however, the focus of the trade shifted from North Africa to the Americas, where plantations and mines required huge amounts of labor. Soon the ports of the Niger Delta became major export centers of human cargo for European merchants. Between 1700 and 1800 alone, about 814,000 captives were loaded onto slave ships there. The Niger Delta region, therefore, was responsible for a sizeable segment of the 5.5 million Africans transported across the Atlantic Ocean during that time.

With the demand for slaves so high, ambitious Igbo were able to prosper at the expense of their fellow Africans by becoming involved in the trade. The most enterprising among these groups

Timber being processed for export by manual laborers in Nigeria. The Igbo economy was traditionally based on the export of crops in exchange for such goods as salt, glass beads, textiles, and metals from their northern neighbors.

35

was the Aro, an important Igbo clan whose members were known for their adventurousness and their skill as traders. Having established trading posts throughout Igboland for the exchange of various goods, the Aro were well positioned to handle the transfer of slaves from Africa's interior to its seaports. As they pursued this industry, they also used an ingenious technique to acquire slaves for their own purposes.

Aro country was home to a famous religious shrine, which people would often visit to communicate with Chukwu, the Creator. During the years of the slave trade, visitors to the shrine were often told that Chukwu was angry with them. According to the Aro priests, the sinners could obtain forgiveness only by making a gift of slaves to Chukwu; when the slaves were turned over to the Aro—free of charge—the Aro promptly sold

A carved dance headdress depicts a slaver in a European hat bringing a woman to the coast for trade. The Igbo practiced slavery on a small scale—trading prisoners of war, criminals, or members of impoverished families—before the vast European slave trade developed in the 17th century.

them to Europeans.

Slave dealers less crafty than the Aro relied on brute force. The more powerful bands raided villages to obtain captives; others patrolled the countryside, kidnapping individuals unfortunate enough to cross their paths.

Among those who fell into the hands of kidnappers was a young boy known as Olaudah Ekwuno. Captured sometime around 1750 and shipped to North America, Ekwuno served successive masters; his changing fortunes took him to Virginia, the West Indies, and England. While serving the captain of a merchant vessel, he earned enough money to purchase his freedom. He then settled in England and earned his living at a variety of occupations, gaining widespread admiration for his intelligence and integrity. Ekwuno later joined the British antislavery movement and helped to establish Freetown, a settlement for liberated slaves on Africa's West Atlantic coast. In 1788, he published his autobiography, *The Interesting Narrative of the Life of Olaudah Equiano, or Gustavus Vassa the African,* a classic indictment of slavery and a moving account of human perseverance.

Unfortunately, the majority of Igbo sold into slavery did not fare as well as Olaudah Ekwuno. Many Igbo communities suffered the loss of able-bodied citizens but received no compensation. Though officially outlawed in 1807, the slave trade continued until the middle of the 19th century, when palm oil replaced human beings as the primary export of the Niger Delta. This change,

(Continued on page 41)

THE ART OF THE SAVANNA

Though the Songhay empire extended its sway over many other West African peoples, including the Mossi, Fulani, and Bambara, these groups always maintained their distinctive languages, beliefs, and arts. During the 400 years since the decline of Songhay, the Sudan's diverse cultures have continued to flourish, producing some of the world's most remarkable artworks.

Brass anklets crafted by the Igbo people in the Niger region.

This brass container, or kuduo, with its crocodile-shaped handle, was used to store valuables, including gold dust. Kuduo were sometimes buried with their owners.

A wooden marionette used in the puppet plays performed by Bamana youths at funerals and other social occasions.

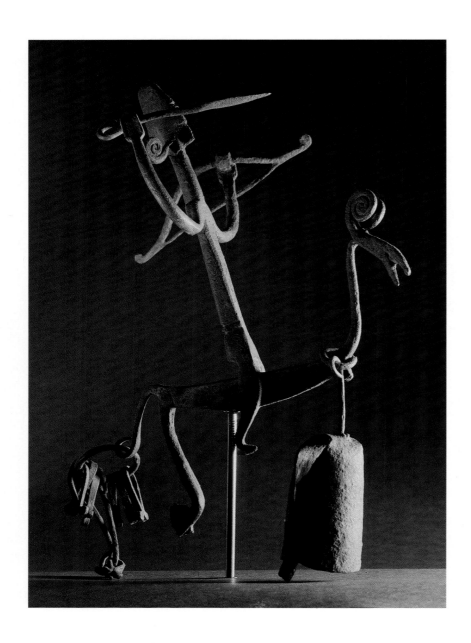

A Mali altar iron in the form of a
stylized horse and armed rider.
Irons such as this one were placed
on the altars of shrines dedicated
to the memory of one's ancestors.

(Continued from page 36)

however, was accompanied by increasing British intrusion, spearheaded by the Royal Niger Company and groups of Christian missionaries. At the end of the century, British troops were brought in to crush Igbo resistance, and Igboland became part of the British colony of Nigeria.

The British preferred to rule their African colonies indirectly through local kings and chiefs. (The French, on the other hand, always replaced African rulers with French officials and considered their colonial possessions part of France.) Because there was no central political authority in Igboland, the British found it very difficult to exercise effective control, and the Igbo remained largely independent. At the same time, many Igbo communities took advantage of British resources, building schools and other facilities. When Nigeria gained its independence in 1960, the Igbo played a leading role in the development of the new nation, the largest and most prosperous in West Africa.

Today the Igbo continue to live in independent villages numbering between a few hundred and 2,000 in population. Though many Igbo have adopted Christianity, the observance of traditional religions continues, as do the time-honored customs of village life. The experiences and achievements of the Igbo in the modern world are perhaps best exemplified in the life and work of Chinua Achebe, the world-renowned Nigerian novelist. In Achebe's 1960 novel *No Longer at Ease*, an elder of the village of Iguedo, noting all the changes he has seen, sums up the unyielding spirit of the Igbo:

> Iguedo breeds great men. . . . When I was young I knew of them—Okonkwo, Ezeudu, Obierika, Okolo, Nwosu. . . . These men were great in their day. Today greatness has changed its tune. Titles are no longer great, neither are barns or large numbers of wives and children. Greatness is now in the things of the white man. And so we too have changed our tune. We are the first in all the nine villages to send our son to the white man's land [to study]. Greatness has belonged to Iguedo from ancient times. It is not made by man. You cannot plant greatness as you plant yams or maize. Who ever planted an oroko tree—the greatest tree in the forest? You may collect all the oroko seeds in the world, open the soil and put them there. It will be in vain. The great tree chooses where to grow and we find it there, so it is with greatness in men.

41

Chapter 4 | KINGDOM OF THE SUN

Masked Mossi priests in ceremonial garb prepare to worship the spirits of nature and of their ancestors. All members of Mossi communities participated in daily religious rituals to secure peace and prosperity for their land.

In the heart of the central Sudan, a vast, mountain-studded plateau covering 30,000 square miles rises 1,500 feet above sea level. The rugged, reddish terrain of the plateau, dotted with stands of trees and shrubbery, provides striking contrasts: dry and dusty between October and May, it turns magically green with the first summer rains, nurturing a variety of crops to feed its inhabitants. For centuries, this striking land has been home to the Mossi, one of Africa's most powerful and successful ethnic groups. "Land is the mother," they have always said. "It fed the ancestors of this generation; it feeds the present generation and its children; and it provides a final resting place for all men."

The Mossi kingdoms emerged some-

time between the 11th and 13th centuries, when horse warriors from neighboring regions invaded the plateau and conquered the native peoples, who had been living in scattered communities without any central authority. By intermarrying with the local inhabitants, the warriors gave rise to a new ethnic group, the Mossi, and established four distinct kingdoms: Ouagadougou (pronounced Wa-ga-DOO-goo) and Tenkodogo in the center, Yatenga to the north, and Fada-N'Gourma to the east.

The Mossi founded their states in a dangerously capricious climate. If the summer rains came late or were sparse, crops would wither in the fields, threatening the very existence of the community. Even when the elements were kind, the shallow soil could be depleted after two or three years of heavy planting. For these reasons, the Mossi continually sought more land to cultivate. This need for expansion resulted in frequent wars with neighboring peoples, and the Mossi had developed a proud military tradition. Whenever their troops marched to battle, heralds would inspire them with words such as these:

> Men! Your ancestors were not slaves. They were men. They were stronger than anyone else. They did not bathe with water; they bathed with blood . . . . Your ancestors were not afraid of anyone; you must not be afraid of anyone. Even if you are killed today, you must march ahead, beat your enemies, and take their villages. You must not be afraid!

Though the Mossi kingdoms were not as large or as wealthy as others in the Sudan, they normally held their own on the battlefield. During the 14th and 15th centuries, Mossi warriors frequently raided the territories of Mali and Songhay, West Africa's greatest empires, even laying siege to such important cities as Walata and Timbuktu. They met their match only when Sunni Ali became emperor of Songhay in 1464. An incomparably fierce and skillful military commander, Sunni Ali drove the Mossi from Songhay territory and put an end to their dreams of expansion. However, neither Sunni Ali nor any other conqueror felt strong enough to attack the Mossi on their lofty plateau.

Safe from outside threats, the Mossi were able to create a remarkably stable and complex political system. Each of the four Mossi kingdoms was headed by a ruler who bore the title *naba*. The kingdoms were divided into districts and villages, each one governed by a chief. A district contained anywhere from 10,000 to 35,000 people; villages contained as few as 50 persons and as many as 5,000, averaging about 500. Each village was in turn divided into wards, and each ward was comprised of several family compounds.

Although the king was the head of state, the district chiefs had a great deal of authority. Because there was no permanent army, the king relied on his district chiefs to provide troops in times of war; they in turn relied on village chiefs for recruits. (Every adult Mossi male was expected to be available for military service.) Thus, while all Mossi honored the supreme power of the monarchy, in everyday life they had a great deal of control over their own affairs. On the most basic level, the eldest member of a

A modern-day district chief of Ouagadougou in Burkina Faso. Without a permanent army, the Mossi king traditionally relied on such chiefs to provide troops during wartime; thus, the chiefs once had significant authority over their people.

Ouagadougou today is a modern city of about 175,000 inhabitants. Though he does not control his nation's affairs, the mogho naba *continues to possess great power in the eyes of his subjects.*

46

clan was responsible for the conduct of his relatives and had the power to punish individuals for theft and other minor offenses; he could even expel them from the compound. More serious crimes were referred to the district chief, who had the power to deliver the death penalty.

In theory, all the Mossi kingdoms had equal standing. Over the course of time,

however, Ouagadougou came to be the largest of the four and played the dominant role in Mossi political affairs. For this reason, the king of Ouagadougou became known as the *mogho naba*, literally "king of the Mossi country"; despite occasional rivalries, the other three kings usually deferred to him.

Underpinning this complex system was the religious faith shared by most members of the community. Mossi religion was based upon two essential elements: worship of ancestors and worship of nature spirits. Like most African peoples, the Mossi recognized nature as a living force on which their survival depended; they had names for the spirits dwelling in the earth, the water, the sky, and the trees, and they conducted numerous rituals to honor these mysterious, powerful beings. Ancestors were equally important because the Mossi believed that the human spirit remained on earth after the death of the body; thus one's ancestors would guide and protect one if shown the proper respect.

Everyone from the king to the most humble farmer was obligated to perform the necessary religious rites. Each night, the king's chief minister publicly beseeched the Mossi ancestors to grant peace and prosperity to the land, and the prayer was repeated by leaders of every level of society.

In Mossi belief, rulers were set apart from the rest of the population because their ancestors had given them a power known as the *nam*, "that force of God that enables one man to control another." Deeply attached to their land and dependent on its bounty, the Mossi regarded their rulers as embodiments of the life-giving force of the sun. Accordingly, the royal palace was viewed as the center of the world.

The palace's west wall contained two small doorways representing the northern and southern tropics, the limits of the sun's yearly journey across the sky; between the doorways was a small mud hut, built into the wall, that symbolized the equator; a third doorway, the "golden door," marked the sun's highest point in the sky.

Each morning, the king appeared on horseback at the west wall to greet his subjects. With his back to the rising sun, he faced the west and looked out upon his domain, just as the sun gazed at the world. The death of the mogho naba was therefore a calamity of immense proportions. The word would spread throughout Mossi country that "the fire has gone out," and a period of gloom and disorder would descend upon the land until the people heard that a new mogho naba had been selected.

Because of their strength, their unity, and their protected location, the Mossi kingdoms were largely immune to the slave trade that disrupted the lives of many West African communities between 1650 and 1850. Not until the late 19th century did Europeans first set eyes on the Mossi states and appreciate their refinement. "From the very first, in Mossi country," stated a Frenchman who visited in 1890, "one feels that one has entered a new land, more peaceful, richer, and more populous [than nearby areas]. . . . The people one meets on the roads are workers on their way to the fields, or are carrying wares to the neighboring market. They are not like the Songhai or the Bobo, who always carry bows on their shoulders."

Unfortunately, the French were not willing to allow the Mossi to remain in this untroubled state. In 1885, the major European powers had agreed to divide Africa into colonies, and French troops were gradually taking control of the western and central Sudan. Led by the mogho naba, the Mossi resisted in the spirit of their proud warrior tradition; but like other West Africans, they found that their bows, lances, and outmoded muskets were no match for modern European weapons. By the beginning of the 20th century, the Mossi domains were part of French West Africa.

European colonialism lasted only a few decades. In 1960 the Mossi kingdoms achieved their independence as part of a new nation, Upper Volta, which changed its name to Burkina Faso in 1983. Though the nation is home to more than 60 ethnic groups— including the Mamprussi, Dagomba, Bobo, Lobi, and Fulani—the Mossi, numbering nearly three million, have remained the nation's dominant force to the present day.

French authorities of the colonial period stripped the district and village chiefs of their power, and they have never regained it. The mogho naba, however, continues to occupy his palace in the center of Ouagadougou (now a modern city of about 175,000 inhabitants). Though he does not control the affairs of the nation, in the eyes of his subjects he continues to possess the nam and to celebrate the ancient traditions that made the Mossi a powerful people. Each Friday morning, for example, the mogho naba appears on horseback outside the western wall of the palace, as his predecessors had done for centuries. Court drummers begin to play, and a royal herald recounts an incident from the distant past, telling of the time when a mogho naba allowed one of his wives to leave the palace for three days in order to visit her family. When she did not return at the appointed time, the enraged king saddled his horse and prepared to fetch her back.

His ministers, fearing that the absence of the mogho naba would bring calamity, pleaded with him to remain at home, and at last he agreed.

The herald's 15-minute tale includes many facts about Mossi history. At the end of the recitation, the mogho naba repeats the action of his ancestor by dismounting and reentering the palace. At this moment the sun returns to its proper place, and peace reigns once again in Mossi country.

49

Chapter 5 | THE CHAIN OF TSOEDE

Though apparently created in Ife, this exquisite copper sculpture came into the possession of the Nupe. Nupe traditions claim that the statue was among the many gifts taken by Tsoede back to his homeland.

Nearing the end of its 2,600-mile journey through West Africa, the mighty Niger River makes a final bend to the south, flowing into the Benue River as it rushes toward the sea. The meeting of the two great waterways forms a wide V shape on the map; nestled into this sharp angle is the land occupied for many centuries by the Nupe.

According to their oral tradition, the Nupe were once forced to serve the more powerful Idah, whose territory lay farther down the Niger. Sometime during the 15th century, a Nupe chief sent his son Tsoede as a slave to the king of Idah, as part of an agreement between the two peoples. As the years passed, the king of Idah grew to love Tsoede and finally adopted him as a son. When the king grew old and realized that he was about to die, he granted the Nupe their freedom and sent Tsoede back home to be the first king of his people. He also gave Tsoede valuable gifts: a bronze canoe manned by 12 Nupe slaves; a number of long brass trumpets called *kakati;* a set of drums decorated with brass bells; and a heavy iron chain, the *egba Tsoede,* which became the principal symbol of the king's power.

Tsoede traveled upriver in his bronze canoe with his 12 loyal companions. Though 60 years old by then, he was still a vigorous and warlike man. Upon arriving home he overthrew the local Nupe chiefs, replaced them with his cohorts, and amassed a mighty army. Tsoede then conquered a number of neighboring peoples and built a royal capital at Gbara on the Kaduna River, which remained the center of the Nupe kingship for 400 years. He is said to have owned 5,555 horses—so many that one of his sons had to found the town of Dokomba, on the other side of the Kaduna, just to accomodate the royal steeds.

Tsoede's new kingdom was destined to flourish. Located at the meeting point of the southern forest belt and the northern savanna, with access to two great waterways, Nupe quickly developed into a trading center where northern and southern products could be exchanged. By charging fees to the many traders who entered Nupe territory, Tsoede amassed great wealth and established a splendid court at Gbara.

Tsoede is said to have ruled for 60 years, until his death at the age of 120. According to oral tradition, 18 successive Nupe kings—bearing the title *etsu*—ascended the throne after Tsoede. These men ruled so well that Nupe remained strong and prosperous while other states rose and fell. Indeed, the kingdom is said to have reached the height of its power under Etsu Ma'azu in the early 19th century.

During Etsu Ma'azu's reign, however, conditions outside Nupe began to change dramatically. By this time, the Fulani Muslims had completed their conquest of the Hausa states, directly north of Nupe, and had established a powerful Islamic empire. While Ma'azu was alive, the Fulani made no move against Nupe. But when the etsu died in 1818, a civil war broke out over succession to the throne and they moved in swiftly. Fulani troops secured the kingship for Ma'azu's nephew Majiya; but when the new king tried to expel his Fulani allies from Nupe, they routed his army. The Fulani allowed Majiya to remain on the throne as their puppet, but the Muslim holy man Mallam Dendo became the true ruler of Nupe.

Like Usuman dan Fodio and the other great Fulani leaders, Mallam Dendo cared little for earthly power and never aspired to the kingship. His son Dzurugi, known as the Red One, had different ideas. When his father died in 1833, Dzurugi installed himself as etsu, taking possession of the Chain of Tsoede and the other royal insignia. Nupe thus officially became an Islamic kingdom. The Muslim rulers shifted the nation's capital to Bida, a former war camp, and soon transformed the town into a thriving city, filled with mosques, palaces, workshops, markets, and impressive houses occupied by traders

52

and court officials.

Few kingdoms in history have boasted so many public officials as did Nupe. The immense size of this group resulted from the measures taken to avoid bloody conflicts over succession to the throne. Under Muslim rule, the kingship rotated among three royal families, each of which had its own palace, estates, and officials. Upon the death of an etsu, the head of the second family, who had borne the title *shaba,* acceded to the throne; the head of the third family, whose title had been *kpotu,* moved up to become shaba, and the leader of the former etsu's family assumed the title of kpotu. Together, the members of all three royal families formed the nobility of Nupe; they were known as *gitsuzi,* "those who will become king." The gitsuzi themselves bore numerous titles, depending on their relation to the head of their particular family. They also inherited one another's homes; since Nupe law forbade noblemen to build new houses, securing a desirable residence often entailed complicated political intrigues.

Beneath the rank of nobility were numerous officers of state, also divided into three classes: military commanders and civil servants; Muslim holy men and

53

judges; and court slaves. Even the court slaves, selected from prisoners of war, varied in rank. The most favored slaves—both at the royal court and in the households of wealthy citizens—often acquired land and livestock and became important citizens in their own right. Their fate was far more enviable than that of the West African captives sold to European traders and shipped to the Americas.

Though the majority of leading officials were male, women also played an important role in the government of

These wooden carved parchment boards from Nupe were used as protective coverings for precious parchment documents such as the Koran. Nupe officially became an Islamic kingdom in 1833, when Mallam Dendo was succeeded by his son Dzurugi.

The British battle for West African territories is depicted in this 1884 engraving. Like the Hausa states to the north and Igbo and Yoruba to the south, Nupe fell under British control by the end of the 19th century.

Nupe. Each royal family had a senior titled woman known as the *sabi*. The sabi sat on the royal council, had her own properties, and commanded her own troops. In lower levels of society, each district and town had its own sabi, who supervised markets and directed labor performed by women, such as pottery and weaving. Nupe's organization was so thorough that a special title (*lelu*) was even bestowed upon suspected witches in the hope that the women's fearsome powers could be put to work for the welfare of the community.

Citizens of Nupe had no difficulty identifying members of different social classes, because dress varied according to status. Members of the nobility always wore blue turbans and were the only Nupe allowed to carry swords and ride horses. Prominent men dressed in trousers and flowing white robes, while workers and peasants usually wore a blue loincloth and a second blue cloth draped over their shoulders. Social relations among different classes were also carefully regulated. Those of equal rank would bow low while exchanging greetings and then lightly touch one another's fingers.

By contrast, a person of lower rank had to bow or kneel when speaking to a superior and would not presume to offer his or her hand; the other party would receive this homage by remaining upright or by bowing only slightly. In the presence of the king, even the highest officials kept their eyes lowered at all times and sat cross-legged with their hands in their laps. It was considered a grave insult to let one's hands touch the ground in the presence of the etsu.

Despite its strictly enforced hierarchy and the power of its armies, Nupe could not withstand the European drive to control Africa. Like the Hausa states to the north and Igbo and Yoruba to the south, Nupe fell under British control by the end of the 19th century and was incorporated into the colony of Nigeria. Although the British broke up the Nupe empire, the royal court at Bida survived both the colonial period and the struggle for Nigerian independence. Though the Nupe etsu is now subject to Nigeria's civilian government, which is centered in the southern city of Lagos, his aura of greatness is undiminished.

The etsu appears in public every morning, dressed completely in white and riding a horse along the walls of his residence. Each Friday, the etsu travels to Bida's principal mosque in an even more impressive ceremony. Witnessed by the anthropologist Siegfried Nadel during the 1930s, this weekly pageant vividly evokes the enduring grandeur of African civilization:

> Envisage this Friday procession: kings and courtiers on horseback, in their sumptuous gowns, the king under the great silken state umbrella, the horses with trappings of silver and beautiful cloth; a bodyguard carrying swords, and police with their staffs, are running ahead, shouting the *Etsu*'s name. . . . Drummers are beating their drums, three mounted trumpeters blow the huge bronze *kakati* in an incessant deafening chorus; with it blend the shrill notes of the *algeita*, the Hausa oboe, while another musician is beating an iron double bell with a wooden stick, shouting and singing at the same time. All streets are lined with people, adults and children, who watch, fascinated, this procession, bearing witness to the impressiveness of this display of royal power.

55

CHRONOLOGY

c. 2,500 B.C.	Ancestors of the Bambara move south as the Sahara Desert begins to dry out; the Igbo begin to farm in the regions east of the Niger River
7th century	Religion of Islam arises in Arabia and quickly sweeps through Middle East and North Africa
c. 750	Kingdom of ancient Ghana begins to flourish in western Sudan
9th century	The Fulani establish themselves in the kingdom of Takrur, becoming the first West African state to adopt Islam; Igbo culture produces artwork in bronze and copper
10th century	Fulani groups settle in Fouta Djallon, Massina, and Fouta Toro
11th-13th centuries	Mossi kingdoms arise in central Sudan
12th century	Groups of Soninke migrate to Bambara country as ancient Ghana dissolves; Bambara begin to organize powerful chiefdoms but fall under control of Mali and Songhay empires
14th-15th centuries	The Mossi raid kingdoms of Mali and Songhay before being driven out by Songhay's Sunni Ali
1481-1514	Under Tengella and Koly, Fulani troops wage victorious military campaigns throughout Senegambia
1531-91	Tsoede reigns as first king of Nupe
1591	Moroccan forces crush Songhay's army; as Songhay empire dissolves, the Bambara emerge as a leading power of the western Sudan

c.1700	Transatlantic slave trade begins to dominate the economy of Igboland; slave trafficking continues for 150 years
1712	Biton Kulibali, king of Segu, leads Bambara warriors in a series of conquests; the Bambara eventually dominate the western Sudan
1725	Fulani jihad erupts in Fouta Djallon
1766-87	Reign of Ngolo Jara as king of Segu; Bambara conquer Jenne and Timbuktu and gain control of middle Niger
1776	Fulani jihad erupts in Fouta Toro
1780s	Fulani leader Ahmadu Sisu conquers Massina, Jenne, and Timbuktu
1787-1808	Reign of Monzon as king of Segu
1804-12	Fulani jihad led by Usuman dan Fodio rages throughout central Sudan; Fulani victory leads to formation of Sokoto Caliphate and Emirate of Gwandu
1818	Fulani intervene in Nupe during civil war, allowing Nupe heir to rule but stripping him of real power; Muslim holy man Mallam Dendo controls Nupe
1833	Dzurugi becomes first official Muslim king of Nupe
1859	Fulani Muslim troops under Umar Tal conquer Segu and make it part of Torodbe empire
1885	European powers agree to divide Africa into spheres of influence
1890-1900	French and British forces take control of sub-Saharan Africa, creating colonies of French West Africa and Nigeria
1945	World War II ends; independence movements begin spreading throughout Africa
1960	Most of West Africa gains independence from colonial rule; new nations cross the boundaries of ancient kingdoms and combine diverse ethnic groups

57

FURTHER READING

Achebe, Chinua. *No Longer at Ease.* New York: Anchor Books, 1960.

_____. *Things Fall Apart.* New York: Anchor Books, 1959.

Banbera, Tayiru. *A State of Intrigue: The Epic of Bamana Segu.* Edited by David C. Conrad. Oxford: Oxford University Press, 1990.

Connah, Graham. *African Civilizations.* Cambridge: Cambridge University Press, 1987.

Davidson, Basil. *Africa in History.* Rev. ed. New York: Collier, 1991.

_____. *The African Genius.* Boston: Little, Brown, 1969.

Davidson, Basil, with F. K. Buah and the advice of J. F. A. Ajayi. *A History of West Africa,* 1000-1800. New rev. ed. London: Longmans, 1977.

Equiano, Olaudah. *Equiano's Travels: His Autobiography.* Abridged and edited by Paul Edwards. Oxford: Heinemann, 1967.

Hammond, Peter B. Yatenga: *Technology in the Culture of a West African People.* New York: Free Press, 1966.

Hull, Richard W. *African Cities and Towns Before the European Conquest.* New York: Norton, 1976.

Imperato, Pascal J. *African Folk Medicine: Practices and Beliefs of the Bambara and Other Peoples.* Baltimore: York Press, 1977.

_____. "The Dance of the Tyi Wara." *African Arts* (Autumn 1970): 8-13, 71-80.

Isichei, Elizabeth. *Igbo Worlds.* Philadelphia: Institute of Human Issues, 1978.

McEvedy, Colin. *The Penguin Atlas of African History.* New York: Penguin, 1980.

Manning, Patrick. *Slavery and African Life.* Cambridge: Cambridge University Press, 1990.

Nadel, Siegfried F. *A Black Byzantium: The Kingdom of Nupe in Nigeria.* London: Oxford University Press, 1942.

Park, Mungo. *Travels in the Interior Districts of Africa.* 1799. Reprint, New York: Arno Press/New York Times, 1971.

St. Croix, F. W. de. *The Fulani of Northern Nigeria.* Farnborough: Gregg International, 1972.

Shaw, Thurstan. *Unearthing Igbo-Ukwu.* London: Oxford University Press, 1977.

Skinner, Elliot P. *The Mossi of the Upper Volta.* Stanford: Stanford University Press, 1964.

Stenning, Derrick J. *Savannah Nomads.* London: Oxford University Press, 1959.

Uchendu, Victor C. *The Igbo of Southeast Nigeria.* New York: Holt, Reinhardt, & Winston, 1965.

UNESCO. General History of Africa. 8 vols. Berkeley: University of California Press, 1980-93.

Webster, J. B., and A. A. Boahen, with M. Tidy. *The Revolutionary Years: West Africa Since 1800.* New ed. London: Longman, 1980.

GLOSSARY

anthropology	the study of human beings, especially in relation to race, culture, and environment
archaeology	the study of the physical remains of past human societies
brass	an alloy (combination) of copper and zinc, widely used by African artisans
bronze	an alloy (combination) of copper and tin, widely used by African artisans
clan	a group of individuals tracing their descent to a common ancestor
colonialism	a political system under which a nation controls another nation or people
hominid	a member of a biological family that includes modern humans and their ancestors
Islam	religion based upon worship of Allah and acceptance of Muhammad as his prophet
jihad	Arabic term meaning "effort"; later used to describe "holy war," the obligation of Muslims to defend Islam against unbelievers and expand its influence
kola	an African nut valued for its stimulant properties; a major item in trade between forest and savanna states

mosque	an Islamic house of worship
Muslim	one who follows the religion of Islam
nomad	member of a group that wanders from place to place, usually in a defined pattern and with the purpose of pasturing animals or securing food
oral tradition	the practice of transmitting stories verbally from one generation to the next rather than writing them down
palm oil	oil extracted from the nuts of African palm trees; a major African export since the 19th century
savanna	landscape distinguished by grasslands and open woodlands; common to West Africa
Sudan	sub-Saharan Africa stretching from the Atlantic coast to the valley of the Nile River; from Bilad al-Sudan, Arabic for "the land of the black peoples"
transatlantic slave trade	traffic in human beings that lasted roughly from 1500 to 1900 and resulted in the shipment of 12 million Africans from their homeland to the Americas
tribute	a payment by one ruler or nation to another as a token of submission or a guarantee of protection
ward	a division of a city created for political or administrative purposes

INDEX

Ahmadu (emperor of Torodbe), 24, 29
Amadu Sisi (Fulani king), 22
Aro (Igbo clan), 35
Art, 25, 37-40
Bambara people, 11-17
   agriculture, 11, 12, 16, 17
   art, 37
   language, 12
   political organization, 12-13
   religion, 11, 17
   warfare, 13-17, 22
Benin, 32, 34
Berber people, 19
Bida, 52, 55
Biton Kulibali (Bambara king), 13-15
Bobo people, 48
British colonialism, 29, 41, 55
Burkina Faso, 29, 48
Chi wara (Bambara god), 11
   ceremony, 11, 17
Chukwu (Igbo god), 33, 35
Dagomba people, 48
Dzurugi (Nupe etsu), 52
Edo people, 32
Emirate of Gwandu, 23, 24, 29
Eze nri, 33-34
Fada-N'Gourma kingdom, 43, 44, 46
Fouta Djallon, 21, 22
Fouta Toro, 21, 22
French colonialism, 17, 29, 41, 48

French West Africa, 17, 29, 48
Fulani people, 19-29, 48
   art, 37
   as cattle herders, 19, 20, 21, 29
   language, 19
   political organization, 23-24
   religion, 20, 21, 22, 23, 24
   warfare, 16-17, 21-29, 52
Fulfulde language, 19
Gambia, 29
Gbara, 51, 52
Ghana empire, 12
Hausa states, 22, 29, 34, 52, 55
Hausa people, 22
Idah people, 51
Igboland, 32-33, 41, 55
Igbo people, 31-41
   agriculture, 32
   language, 31
   political organization, 31-33
   religion, 33-34, 41
   slave trade, 34-37
   warfare, 37-41
Interesting Narrative of the Life of Olaudah Equiano, or Gustavus Vassa the African, The, 36
Islam, 16, 20, 21, 22, 24, 52, 55. *See also* Muslims
Jihads, 16, 22, 23
Koly (Fulani king), 21

Lobi people, 48
Ma'azu (Nupe etsu), 52
Majiya (Nupe etsu), 52
Mali empire, 12, 15, 21, 44
Mamprussi people, 48
Mande language family, 12
Mandingo people, 21, 22
Massina, 21, 22
Monzon (Bambara king), 15-16
Mossi people, 43-49
   agriculture, 43-44
   art, 37
   political organization, 44-46
   religion, 43, 46-47, 48-49
   warfare, 43, 44, 48
Muhammad Bello (Fulani king), 23
Muslims, 16, 22, 23, 34, 52, 53, 55.
   See also Islam
Ngolo Jara (Bambara king), 15
Niger River, 12, 13, 15, 17, 23, 32,
   34, 51
Nigeria, 29, 31, 41, 55
No Longer at Ease (Achebe), 41
North Africa, 12, 34
Nupe people, 51-55
   political organization, 51-52, 53-55
   warfare, 52
Ouagadougou kingdom, 43, 44, 46, 48
Park, Mungo, 15-16
Sahara Desert, 19, 20

Segu, 13, 15-16, 17, 24
Serer people, 19
Shehu, The. *See* Usuman dan Fodio
Slavery, 12, 34-36, 44, 51, 54
Slave trade, 34-36, 47
Sokoto Caliphate, 22-23, 24, 29
Songhay empire, 12, 15, 21, 37, 44
Soninke people, 12
Sudan, 22, 23, 37, 43, 44, 48
Sunni Ali (emperor of Songhay), 21,
   44
Tayiru Banbera, 12, 15
Tengella (Fulani king), 21
Tenkodogo kingdom, 43, 44, 46
Timbuktu, 15, 44
Torodbe Empire, 23-29
Tsoede (Nupe etsu), 51-52
   Chain of, 51, 52
Tuareg people, 22
Umar Tal (emperor of Torodbe), 16,
   23-24
Upper Volta, 48
Usuman dan Fodio (Fulani king), 22-
   23, 52
West Africa, 12, 16, 20, 22, 23, 41,
   44, 51
Wolof people, 19, 22
Yatenga kingdom, 43, 44, 46
Yorubaland, 32, 34, 55
Yoruba people, 32

PHILIP KOSLOW earned his B.A. and M.A. degrees from New York University and went on to teach and conduct research at Oxford University, where his interest in medieval European and African history was awakened. In addition to writing the preceding 11 volumes of THE KINGDOMS OF AFRICA, he is the author of *El Cid* in the Chelsea House series HISPANICS OF ACHIEVEMENT and of *Centuries of Greatness: The West African Kingdoms, 750-1900* in Chelsea House's MILESTONES IN BLACK AMERICAN HISTORY series.

PICTURE CREDITS

Every effort has been made to contact the copyright owners of photographs and illustrations used in this book. In the event that the holder of a copyright has not heard from us, he or she should contact Chelsea House Publishers.

page

2: The Metropolitan Museum of Art, Gift of Mr. and Mrs. Charles Mann, 1984. (1984.127)
6: illustration by Gary Tong
8: Werner Forman/Art Resource, NY
10: Musee De L'Homme, photo by P. Verger
13: Werner Forman/Art Resource, NY
14-15: United Nations
18: Werner Forman/Art Resource, NY
20: United Nations
23: Art Resource, NY
24: Musee De L'Homme

Color Section
25: Musee De L'Homme
26: Werner Forman Archive, Private Collection, London
27: (l) Werner Forman Archive, Dallas Museum of Arts (formerly Schindler Collection), (r) Musee De L'Homme, photo by D. Ponsard
28: Musee De L'Homme

30: "Unearthing Igbo-Ukwu, an account of Archaeology in Eastern Nigeria," 1970
32: Werner Forman/Art Resource, NY
35: United Nations/DPI Photo
36: Werner Forman/Art Resource, NY

Color Section
37: Aldo Tutino/Art Resource, NY
38: Werner Forman Archive, Musee Royal de l'Afrique Cenrrale, Tervuren
39: Werner Forman Archive, Dallas Museum of Arts (formerly Schindler Collection)
40: Werner Forman Archive, Courtesy Entwistle Gallery, London

42: "General History of Africa," vol. VI
45: Musee De L'Homme
46: United Nations
50: Werner Forman Archive, National Museum, Lagos, Nigeria
53: Staatliche Museen zu Berlin-PreuBischer Kulturbesitz, Museum fur Volkerkunde, photo by Dietrich Graf
54: Culver Pictures, Inc.